THE WORLD'S GREATEST
TANKS

Ian Graham

Raintree

Chicago, Illinois

© Copyright 2006 Raintree
Published by Raintree,
a division of Reed Elsevier Inc.
Chicago, IL 60602

Customer Service 888-363-4266
Visit our website at
www.heinemannraintree.com

For more information address the publisher:
Raintree, 100 N. LaSalle, Suite 1200, Chicago,
IL 60602

Editorial: Andrew Farrow and Dan Nunn
Design: Ron Kamen and Philippa Baile
Picture Research: Hannah Taylor and Elaine
 Willis
Production: Duncan Gilbert

Originated by Dot Gradations Ltd.
Printed in China

The paper used to print this book comes from
sustainable resources.

10 09 08 07 06
10 9 8 7 6 5 4 3 2

Library of Congress Cataloging-in-Publication Data

Graham, Ian, 1953-
  Tanks / Ian Graham.
    p. cm. -- (The world's greatest)
  Includes bibliographical references and
  index.
  ISBN 1-4109-2087-9 (lib. bdg : alk. paper) --
  ISBN 1-4109-2094-1 (pbk. : alk. paper)
  1. Tanks (Military science)--Juvenile
  literature.
  2. Armored vehicles, military--Juvenile
  literature.
  I. Title. II. Series.

UG446.5.G6828 2005
623.7'4752--dc22
                    2005016355

Acknowledgments

The publishers would like to thank the
following for permission to reproduce
photographs:

AKG pp. **8** (ullstein – Fotoagentur imo),
16 (ullstein – SV-Bilderdienst), **19**
(ullstein – SV-Bilderdienst); Associated Press
pp. **21**, **23**; Corbis pp. **9 top** (Reuters/Alexei
Vladykin), **9 bottom** (Robin Adshead/The
Military Picture Library), **13** (Bettmann),
22 (Reuters/Richard Chung); Corbis Sygma
p. **10** (Gyori Antoine); General Dynamics Land
Systems p. **25 bottom**; Getty Images pp. **4 left**
(Hulton Archive), **4 right** (Time Life Pictures),
5, **6** (Time Life Pictures), **11 bottom** (AFP),
18 (Hulton Archive), **20** (AFP), **24** (Time
Life Pictures); Imperial War Museum p. **17**;
Repaircraft PLC pp. **1**, **12**; Reuters p. **11 top**
(Kim Kyung-Hoon); Swedish Defence Images
pp. **14** (Lasse Siogren), **15** (Lasse Siogren);
United States Department of Defence p. **25 top**.

Cover photograph of an M1-A2 Abrams tank
reproduced with permission of Getty Images/
Time Life Pictures.

ISBN 978-1-4109-2087-4 (HC)
ISBN 978-1-4109-2094-2 (PBK)

Contents

Tanks..................................4

The World's Best Tank.......................6

Other Main Battle Tanks......................8

A Different Tank Design.....................10

The Fastest Tank........................12

The Strangest Tank......................14

The Heaviest Tank.......................16

The Greatest Tank of World War II.............18

The Most Popular Tank...................20

Other Popular Tanks...................22

Tanks in Action......................24

Facts and Figures....................26

Glossary..........................28

Further Information................30

Index.........................32

Words appearing in the text in bold, **like this**, are explained in the Glossary.

Tanks

The tank is a powerful weapon of war. It has a big gun that can destroy other tanks and vehicles. The gun is in a **turret** that can turn and point in any direction.

What are tanks for?

At first, soldiers used tanks to help them attack enemy soldiers. Tanks moved forward as the soldiers took cover behind them. When the tanks reached the enemy, the soldiers did the fighting. Soon afterward, tanks began to fight other tanks.

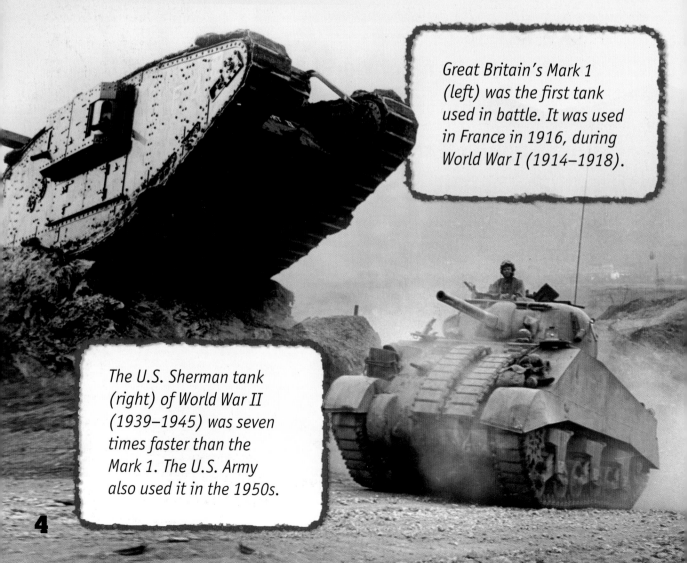

Great Britain's Mark 1 (left) was the first tank used in battle. It was used in France in 1916, during World War I (1914–1918).

The U.S. Sherman tank (right) of World War II (1939–1945) was seven times faster than the Mark 1. The U.S. Army also used it in the 1950s.

Tanks can cover ground fast in desert warfare.

Taking the weight

Tanks have a thick, heavy **armor** to protect the crew. Tanks would sink into soft ground if they had wheels like other vehicles. Instead, they have **tracks**—one on each side. Tracks spread a tank's weight evenly over the ground. This stops it from sinking.

Steering

A tank cannot turn its tracks to turn a corner. A tank turns by slowing down or stopping one of its tracks. It acts like a brake on that side of the tank. The other track keeps going and pushes the tank round.

WORLD TANKS

There are more than 110,000 tanks used by armies all over the world.

	Mark I	M4 Sherman
Used In:	World War I	World War II
Crew:	8	5
Top Speed:	4 mph/6 kph	26 mph/42 kph
Weight:	62,720 lb./28,450 kg	69,565 lb./31,555 kg
Armament:	Two 6 pound guns and four **machine guns**	A 75 mm main gun, three machine guns, and a 2 inch **mortar**

The World's Best Tank

The world's most advanced tank is the United States M1 Abrams. It is designed to be able to destroy any other tank. The latest model is the M1A2. The M1A2 is nearly twice as heavy as a freight truck. It is almost three times as powerful.

Inside the Abrams

The Abrams tank has a crew of four soldiers. The **commander** is in charge. The commander sits in the turret. The **gunner** sits in front of the commander. The gunner aims and fires the gun. The **loader** sits beside the commander and loads the gun. The driver sits at the front of the tank.

The Abrams tank is very low to the ground. This makes it hard to shoot at.

Jet power

Most tanks have **diesel engines**, like those used by road trucks. The Abrams tank has a **gas turbine engine**. It works like the jet engine of a fighter plane. It is as powerful as ten car engines!

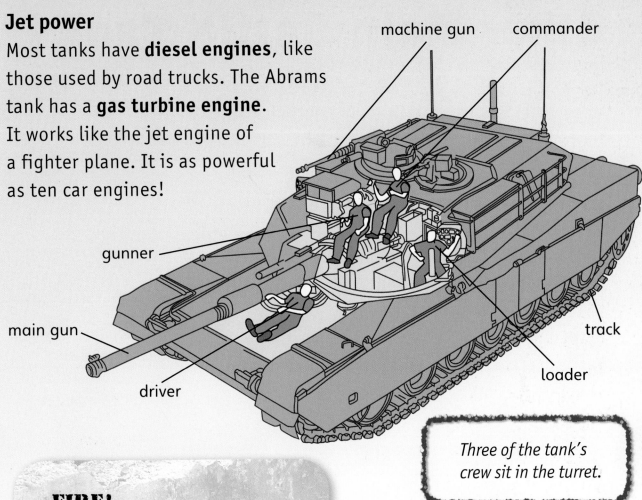

machine gun   commander

gunner

main gun

driver

track

loader

Three of the tank's crew sit in the turret.

FIRE!

The Abrams tank uses a laser and computers to fire its **main gun** very accurately. It can hit targets more than two miles (four kilometers) away.

	Abrams tank	Road truck
Crew:	4	1
Engine Power:	1,500 horsepower	Up to 600 horsepower
Engine Type:	Gas turbine	Diesel
Weight:	155,770 lb./70,655 kg	Up to 80,000 lb./36,285 kg
Armament:	120 mm main gun and 3 machine-guns	None

Other Main Battle Tanks

Many other countries have **main battle tanks**. These include Germany's Leopard 2, Great Britain's Challenger 2, and the Russian T-90.

Leopard tracks

The Leopard 2 has a diesel engine as powerful as the engine in the United States Abrams tank. That makes it very fast for a battle tank. New Leopard 2 tanks have a gun with a longer **barrel**. It lets the Leopard 2 hit targets further away, up to 3 miles (5,000 meters).

The Leopard 2's engine can be taken out for repair or replacement in only 15 minutes.

	Challenger 2	**Leopard 2**	**T-90**
Crew:	4	4	3
Top Speed:	37 mph/60 kph	45 mph/72 kph	37 mph/60 kph
Weight:	137,790 lb./62,500 kg	136,685 lb./62,000 kg	102,515 lb./46,500 kg
Armament:	120 mm main gun and 2 machine guns	120 mm main gun and 2 machine guns	125 mm main gun and 2 machine guns

Missile tank

The T-90 is the latest of Russia's main tanks. It has a 125 millimeter gun, which is bigger than most other tank guns today. This size gun lets the tank fire a guided **missile** out of the tank's main gun. Using the missile, the T-90 can even attack helicopters!

Great Britain's Challenger

The Challenger 2 tank has an unusual gun. It has grooves on the inside of the barrel. These make **shells** spin as they fly through the air. This makes them more accurate. The barrels of most tank guns are smooth inside. They do not make shells spin.

Computers keep the Challenger 2's gun pointing at its target. This means the gun can fire accurately even when the tank is racing over rough ground.

A Different Tank Design

Israel's Merkava tank is different from most other tanks. It has a very interesting design.

Engine at the front

Tanks usually have their engine at the back. The Merkava is the only big battle tank that has its engine at the front. This gives the crew extra protection, like an extra layer of armor.

The Merkava's turret has a very sloping shape to deflect shells that hit it.

Merkava Mark 4

Crew:	**4**
Weight:	**143,300 lb./65,000 kg**
Top Speed:	**37 mph/60 kph**
Armament:	**120 mm main gun, 3 machine guns and a 60 mm mortar**

The Merkava has a door, called a hatch, in the back.

hatch

Safety first

Tank crews get in and out of their tanks through small doors in the top of the **turret**. But it is very dangerous to climb on top of a tank when the enemy might shoot at it. The Merkava has a door at the back. This means that its crew can get in and out while taking cover behind the tank.

Carrying troops

The Merkava can also fit eight soldiers inside. It is the only tank in the world that can do this. It does not normally carry extra soldiers, but in an emergency it could rescue the crew of another tank.

The Merkava carries 50 rounds of ammunition for its main gun, more than most other tanks.

The Fastest Tank

Great Britain's Scorpion tank holds the world record speed for a modern tank—51.1 mph (82.2 kph). The Scorpion is a light tank. It is smaller than main battle tanks like the United States Abrams. The crew is protected by light armor made from aluminium. Scorpions can be powered by a Jaguar sports car engine or a bigger diesel engine.

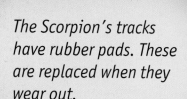

The Scorpion's tracks have rubber pads. These are replaced when they wear out.

Scorpion Light Tank

Crew:	3
Weight:	17,800 lb./8,075 kg
Top Speed:	51.1 mph/82.2 kph
Armament:	76 mm main gun and one machine gun

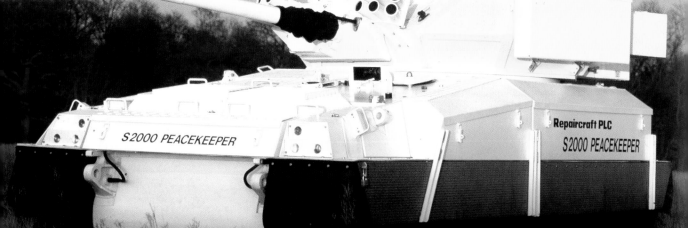

Speedy Peacekeeper

The tank that set the speed record is a version of the Scorpion called the S2000 Peacekeeper. It has a diesel engine. It set the record on March 26, 2002. Speed records are usually set on racetracks, but tank tracks would damage a normal racetrack. This record was set on a special test track in England. If the track had been longer, the tank could have gone even faster!

SPEED MACHINES

◎ In the 1930s, the United States T3 Christie tank reached the amazing speed of 70 mph (112 kph).
◎ The biggest battle tanks are much heavier than the Scorpion and so they are slower. The Leopard 2 is one of the fastest, at 45 mph (72 kph).

This version of the United States T3 Christie tank from the 1930s is unusual. It doesn't have a turret!

The Strangest Tank

Tank designers try to make tanks low so that enemies have a small target to shoot at. The Swedish Stridsvagn Strv-103 was made low and flat by having no turret. The gun is fixed on the tank's flat top. It cannot turn or tilt at all!

The Stridsvagn Strv-103 is also called the S-tank.

Stridsvagn Strv-103

Crew:	3
Weight:	93,710 lb./42,500 kg
Top Speed:	30 mph/50 kph
Armament:	105 mm main gun and machine gun

Turn and tilt

A tank's turret turns so that the gun can point in any direction. The gun can also be tilted up or down, so that the shell flies the right distance to the target. The Strv-103 has to have a way of doing the same thing with a gun that does not turn or tilt.

If the gun cannot move, then the whole tank has to move to take aim. First, the tank turns to point the gun in the right direction. Then, the whole tank tilts up or down. But this way of aiming causes problems. Most tanks can aim and fire while they are moving. The Strv-103 has to stop first. And when the tank tilts up, the enemy has a bigger target to fire at. So, no more tanks like the Strv-103 have been built.

For a Strv-103 to take aim, the whole tank has to turn and tilt to fire the gun.

The Heaviest Tank

During World War II (1939–1945), some tank designers tried to build unstoppable tanks. They made tanks that had a huge gun with very thick armor. This armor made the tanks very big and heavy. These super-tanks were so heavy that they were extremely slow.

Mighty Maus

In 1943, Germany produced a tank called the Maus, which means "mouse." It weighed an amazing 207 tons (more than 400,000 pounds). That's more than twice the weight of the heaviest tank today, the United States M1A2 Abrams. It was so slow that you could pedal a bicycle faster! The Maus had a 5 inch (128 millimeter) main gun. This was far bigger than other tank guns of that time.

Germany's Maus tank was built in 1943. In this photo, the gun is hidden behind the turret.

The armored tortoise

The heaviest British tank was the A39 Tortoise. It was built in the 1940s, like the German Maus. The Tortoise was so heavy that no tank transporter of the day could carry it. In fact, it could hardly move by itself either! The Tortoise was cancelled soon after testing.

The German Maus tank was three times the weight of today's Challenger 2 tank.

The Tortoise tank had the biggest gun of any British tank in the 1940s. The Tortoise was a failure because it was so heavy and slow.

	Maus	**A39 Tortoise**
Crew:	6	7
Weight:	414,470 lb./188,000 kg	174,720 lb./79,252 kg
Top Speed:	12 mph/20 kph	12 mph/20 kph
Armament:	128 mm main gun plus 75 mm gun and a 20 mm cannon	94 mm main gun and 3 machine guns

The Greatest Tank of World War II

The Soviet Union's T-34 tank fought in World War II (1939–1945). It was very advanced for the 1940s. It was fast, even on rough ground. It had thick armor. And it was equal in firepower to any other tank. The Soviet Union's enemy, Germany, had to build better tanks to match it.

Sloping armor

The T-34 had sloping sides. These made it harder to destroy the tank. When shells hit its sloping armor, some of them just bounced off. And when the T-34 was damaged, it was quick and easy to repair.

The T-34 tank was better than the enemy tanks it faced in 1941.

Keeping up with the enemy

At first, the T-34 was armed with a 3 inch (76 millimeter) gun. Soon, new German tanks like the Panther could match it, so a better T-34 was built. It had a bigger 3.3 inch (85 millimeter) gun. The new tank was called the T-34/85.

The German Panther tank was built to match the Soviet T-34.

	T34/76	T-34/85	Panther
Crew:	4	5	5
Weight:	59,085 lb./26,800 kg	70,550 lb./32,000 kg	98,767 lb./44,800 kg
Top Speed:	34 mph/55 kph	34 mph/55 kph	29 mph/46 kph
Armament:	76 mm main gun and 1 machine gun	85 mm main gun and 2 machine guns	75 mm main gun and 2 machine guns

The Most Popular Tank

About 50,000 T-72 tanks have been built since 1972. Nearly 30 armies around the world have used it. Over that long time, it has had new guns, more powerful engines, thicker armor, and the latest electronics.

Cutting the crew

The T-72 needs a crew of only three soldiers instead of the usual four. Most tanks have a loader, whose job is to load the gun. The T-72's main gun loads itself, so the loader is not needed.

The T-72 tank has been built in great numbers.

Exploding armor!

In the 1980s, the T-72 got a new type of armor. It is called **Explosive** Reactive Armor (ERA), because it is designed to explode! Exploding armor might seem like a crazy idea, but there is a good reason for using it. One type of **ammunition** used against tanks sends a jet of hot metal through the tank's armor. Exploding armor stops the jet from cutting through the tank.

T-72

Crew: **3**
Weight: **98,105 lb./44,500 kg**
Top Speed: **37 mph/60 kph**
Armament: **125 mm main gun and 2 machine guns**

Some T-72 tanks were fitted with Explosive Reactive Armor (ERA). It looks like thick flat tiles bolted onto the top of the tank.

Other Popular Tanks

The United States M60 Patton tank was the country's main battle tank for 20 years before the Abrams tank replaced it. It was used by the armies of 22 countries.

Missile tank

The M60 was updated three times to make it better. The first update was called the M60A1. It had a new slimmer turret and thicker armor. The next update was the M60A2. It had a much bigger gun that could fire missiles as well as normal ammunition. The M60A2 did not work very well. The missile system made it too complicated.

The M60 tank was a very successful design. More than 15,000 M60 tanks were built.

Third time is a charm

The final update was the M60A3. It was the best and most successful. The missile system was taken out. The latest computer for aiming the main gun was installed. The M60A3 could be driven over obstacles nearly a 3 feet (1 meter) high. It could cross gaps 8 feet 6 inches (2.6 meters) wide.

> Israel's Sabra tank was developed from the M60.

	M60A3	Sabra
Crew:	4	4
Weight:	114,000 lb./51,700 kg	123,200 lb./55,880 kg
Top Speed:	30 mph/48 kph	30 mph/48 kph
Armament:	105 mm main gun and 2 machine guns	120 mm main gun and 3 machine guns

Tanks in Action

Tanks have to fight on all sorts of ground. They can go fastest on roads, but they are more likely to be travelling across the countryside. They may have to cross soft ground or desert sand, or climb steep slopes. They may also have to go through water.

Crossing water

Most tanks can go through water from 2 to 6 feet (1 to 3 meters) deep. Some tanks can go through deeper water by using snorkels. A snorkel is a long pipe that fits on top of a tank so that air can get in. The engine needs a snorkel too, to let air in and waste gas out. The Russian T-80 tank can go through water 16 feet (5 meters) deep by using snorkels.

Snorkels are used when tanks need to travel through very deep water.

Rescue tanks

Tanks sometimes break down and have to be rescued. Another tank makes the best recovery vehicle. A rescue tank does not need a gun. Instead, the **hull** has a crane on top. Other vehicles based on tanks include armored bulldozers, bridge-laying tanks, and tanks that clear mine-fields.

A bridge-laying tank can put down a folding metal bridge over a river in just a few minutes.

Facts and Figures

There are dozens of types of tanks. Some of them are listed here. You can use the information to see which tanks are the biggest and heaviest, which have the biggest guns, and which are the fastest. Can you see how tank guns have got bigger over the years?

If you want to know more about these or other tanks, look on pages 30 and 31 to find out how to do some research.

WORLD WAR I TANKS (1914–1918)

Tank	Total Length	Weight	Top Speed	Main Gun
A7V Battle Tank (Germany)	24 ft. 1 in./7.3 m	65,920 lb./29,900 kg	5 mph/8 kph	57 mm
Mark 1 (UK)	32 ft. 6 in./9.9 m	62,720 lb./28,450 kg	4 mph/6 kph	Two 6 pounders

WORLD WAR II TANKS (1939–1945)

Tank	Total Length	Weight	Top Speed	Main Gun
A22 Churchill I (UK)	24 ft. 5 in./7.4 m	87,360 lb./39,575 kg	15 mph/25 kph	2 pounder
A27 Cromwell (UK)	20 ft. 10 in./6.4 m	61,600 lb./27,940 kg	40 mph/64 kph	6 pounder
A39 Tortoise (UK)	33 ft. 2 in./10.1 m	174,720 lb./79,252 kg	12 mph/20 kph	32 pounder
M3 Grant (USA)	18 ft. 6 in./5.6 m	60,000 lb./27,215 kg	26 mph/42 kph	75 mm
KV-1 (Russia)	20 ft. 7 in./6.3 m	104,720 lb./47,500 kg	22 mph/35 kph	76 mm
M4 Sherman (USA)	20 ft. 7 in./6.3 m	69,565 lb./31,555 kg	26 mph/42 kph	75 mm or 17 pounder
Maus (Germany)	33 ft. 2 in./10.1 m	414,470 lb./188,000 kg	12 mph/20 kph	128 mm
PzKpfw V Panther (Germany)	22 ft. 6 in./6.7 m	98,765 lb./44,800 kg	29 mph/46 kph	75 mm
PzKpfw VI Tiger I (Germany)	27 ft./8.3 m	121,255 lb./55,000 kg	24 mph/38 kph	88 mm
PzKpfw VI Tiger II (Germany)	33 ft. 9 in./10.3 m	153,000 lb./69,400 kg	24 mph/38 kph	88 mm
T-34/85 (Soviet Union)	26 ft. 11 in./8.2 m	70,550 lb./32,000 kg	34 mph/55 kph	85 mm

MODERN TANKS

Tank	Total Length	Weight	Top Speed	Main Gun
Ariete (Italy)	31 ft. 9 in./9.7 m	119,050 lb./54,000 kg	40 mph/65 kph	120 mm
Challenger 2 (UK)	37 ft. 9 in./11.5 m	137,790 lb./62,500 kg	37 mph/60 kph	120 mm
K1/A1 (Korea)	31 ft. 10 in./9.7 m	120,150 lb./54,500 kg	40 mph/65 kph	120 mm
Leclerc (France)	32 ft. 6 in./9.9 m	123,459 lb./56,000 kg	43 mph/70 kph	120 mm
Leopard 2 (Germany)	31 ft. 9 in./9.7 m	136,685 lb./62,000 kg	45 mph/72 kph	120 mm
M1A2 Abrams (USA)	32 ft. 3 in./9.8 m	155,770 lb./70,655 kg	42 mph/68 kph	120 mm
M60A3 (USA)	30 ft. 10 in./9.4 m	114,000 lb./51,700 kg	30 mph/48 kph	105 mm
Merkava Mark 4 (Israel)	29 ft. 7 in./9.0 m	143,300 lb./65,000 kg	37 mph/60 kph	120 mm
Olifant (South Africa)	33 ft. 6 in./10.2 m	127,870 lb./58,000 kg	37 mph/60 kph	105 mm
Sabra (Israel)	30 ft. 10 in./9.4 m	123,200 lb./55,880 kg	30 mph/48 kph	120 mm
Scorpion light tank (UK)	15 ft. 8 in./4.8 m	17,800 lb./8,075 kg	50 mph/80 kph	76 mm
Stridsvagn Strv-103 (Sweden)	29 ft. 6 in./9.0 m	93,710 lb./42,500 kg	30 mph/50 kph	105 mm
T-72 (Russia)	31 ft. 3 in./9.5 m	98,105 lb./44,500 kg	37 mph/60 kph	125 mm
T-80 (Russia)	31 ft. 8 in./9.7 m	101,415 lb./46,000 kg	43 mph/70 kph	125 mm
T-90 (Russia)	31 ft. 3 in./9.5 m	102,515 lb./46,500 kg	37 mph/60 kph	125 mm
Type 90 (Japan)	32 ft./9.8 m	110,000 lb./50,000 kg	43 mph/70 kph	120 mm
Type 90-II (China)	33 ft./10.1 m	105,820 lb./48,000 kg	40 mph/65 kph	125 mm

Armor

Tank armor has to be tough enough to protect tank crews. At first, thick metal armor was used. When tanks were fitted with bigger guns, the armor was made thicker. But armor is very heavy. So designers looked for new ways of protecting tanks without using thicker metal. Modern tank armor is top secret. Some is made from a "sandwich" of metal and plastic. Armor made from different materials like this is called composite armor.

Future tanks

Tanks could be made a lot smaller, and harder to attack, if they did not have people inside them. So, future tanks may have no crews inside! The driver could sit in a control room, looking at a video screen. When the driver moves his controls, radio signals would make the tank move.

Glossary

ammunition bullets or shells that can be fired from a gun

armor thick metal used to protect a tank crew from attack

barrel the long, tube-shaped part of a tank's gun, which shells are fired through

commander crew member in charge of a tank. The commander decides where the tank should go and what it should shoot at.

diesel engine type of engine used by most tanks. Diesel engines are named after their inventor, Rudolf Diesel.

explosive substance that bursts out with a great force and noise. The shells fired by tanks are filled with explosives.

gas turbine engine type of engine used by the United States Abrams tank. Fuel burned inside the engine heats air. Air expands as it heats up. The force of the air spins a turbine, like wind blowing a windmill but much faster. The spinning turbine drives the tank's tracks.

gunner member of a tank's crew who aims and fires the gun

hull main body of a tank

loader member of a tank's crew who loads the main gun. The loader also takes out the empty shell cases after the gun has been fired.

machine gun type of gun that fires very quickly

main battle tank (MBT) a country's most important type of tank. MBTs form most of a country's tank force.

main gun a tank's biggest gun

missile weapon that is powered by a rocket. It flies toward its target and explodes.

mortar short wide tube used to fire shells high in the air, to drop on nearby targets

shell metal case shaped like a bullet, which is full of explosives. It is fired from a large gun and explodes when it hits something.

track continuous metal belt, like a flattened bicycle chain, that goes around a tank's wheels. Tracks spread a tank's great weight over the ground so that it doesn't sink. The track links grip the ground better than a tire.

turret top part of a tank where the main gun is located. The turret turns round so that the gun can point in any direction.

Further Information

You can find out more information about military vehicles and tanks by reading the following books about these subjects.

Books to read

Here are some more books about tanks:

Cornish, Geoff. *Tanks (Military Hardware in Action)*. Minneapolis: Lerner Publishing, Inc., 2003.

Graham, Ian. *Designed for Success: Military Vehicles*. Chicago: Heinemann Library, 2004.

Green, Michael, and Greg Stewart. *Modern U.S. Tanks & AFVs*. Osceola, Wisconsin: Motorbooks International, 2003.

Places to visit

Do you know how the first tanks were invented and where? You can learn more about tanks by visiting these museums and experiencing what it is like to be in a tank.

American Armoured Foundation Tank Museum

Located in Danville, Virginia, this museum has a collection of military tanks and artifacts.

Eldred World War II Museum

The town of Eldred, Pennsylvania was the site of a munitions plant that made artillery for Great Britain and the United States during World War II. The museum houses an authentic U.S. M551 Sheridan Tank, which was donated by the U.S. Army.

Index

A7V 26
Abrams 6, 7, 12, 16, 22, 27
Ariete 27
armor 5, 10, 12, 18, 21, 22, 27

bridge-laying tanks 25
bulldozer 25

Challenger 8, 9, 27
Christie 13
Churchill 26
commander 6
Cromwell 26

driver 6

engines 7, 8, 10, 12, 13, 20, 24
explosive reactive armor 21

future tanks 27

Grant 26
gunner 6, 7

hull 25

KV-1 26
K1/A1 27

Leclerc 27
Leopard 8, 13, 27
loader 6, 7, 20

Mark 1 4, 5, 26
Maus 16, 17, 26
Merkava 10, 11, 27
mine-clearance tanks 25

Olifant 27

Panther 19, 26
Patton 22

recovery vehicles 25

Sabra 23, 27
Scorpion 12, 13, 27
Sherman 4, 5, 26
snorkel 24
steering 5
Stridsvagn 14, 15, 27

Tiger 26
T-34 18, 19, 26
T-72 20, 21, 27
T-80 24, 27
T-90 8, 9, 27
Tortoise 17
tracks 5, 12, 13
turret 4, 6, 7, 10, 13, 14, 15, 22
Type 90 27
Type 90-II 27